DATING WITH A DESTINATION

OMAR BOGAN

Dedication

To my big sister Aileen for loving me and always having my best interest at heart, thank you so much! My godmother Ms. Adrienne Cozart for keeping me straight on those talks when I needed to listen to my heart and not my head. My brother William O'Neal for restoring my faith in marriage and my desire to be happy once more. My godfather Pastor Charles Hankson for being a spiritual father who keeps it real at all times, no matter what. I thank you all for being who you are and always being true to me. I love you all so much and even more grateful to have you all in my life!

TABLE OF CONTENTS

Introduction...2

Section One: Unapologetically Self-Centered...........5

Break Up & Break Down.......................................6

Chapter One: Self-Awareness..............................9

Chapter Two: Self-Reflection 19

Chapter Three: Self-Realization 29

Section Two: A Man's World... Or Not..............40

Set Standards Or Settle.....................................41

Chapter Four: Good & Grown............................45

Chapter Five: To Be Loved By You....................55

Chapter Six: Marks Of Maturity........................65

Chapter Seven: 5 Levels Of Relationships 76

Section Three: We Could Be Us.......................87

Introduction...88

Chapter Eight: Love's Makeup..........................92

Chapter Nine: Relationship Allowance............102

Chapter Eleven: The Truth About Toxicity 112

Chapter Twelve: Getting It Right With Mr. Right.....122

Before You Go…...133

About The Author..137

DATING WITH A
DESTINATION

INTRODUCTION

Oh, hey! Thanks for dropping in. I don't mean to be presumptuous, but you *are* here because of either B or G, right? Notice I said here because of them rather than about them. Let's not play coy. The reality is we all have felt the disappointment of a relationship or situationship that fell short of our expectations. Long after tear-stained pillowcases dry and demolished emotional walls are reconstructed, thoughts of could've, would've, and should've remain. We often reserve our gaze for looking back without creating time and space to look within.

You are here because B, G, or both, depending on personal preference, dropped the ball on the way to happily ever after. I am here because I have been there, done that, and learned a thing or two in the process. My aim for writing *Dating with a Destination* is to ensure that you become enlightened, elevated, and equipped to engage in the long-lasting love affair of your dreams.

Have a seat while I break this thing all the way down. When our time here comes to a close, you will be far more aware of who you are, where things went wrong in the past, who you truly want and need in your future, as well as have an understanding of how to confidently secure the love of your life. But first, let's get back to B and G.

B (short for Boy, Bryant, ex-Boo, or whatever you choose to call him) is your everyday 'round the way kind of guy. He may not turn every lady's head, but he won't make your nose flare in disgust either. You can catch him on the court trash-talking with friends or looking for love in all the wrong places. Superficial he is not. B isn't moved by what's trending. He likes what he likes with no apologies when it comes to clothes, cars, and women. Women! Material things fall in line with your cash flow. The opposite sex is a little trickier. For this reason, B seems to stay with a losing hand. As troubled as his tumultuous past, he is hopeful for the future, anxious even, when it comes to love and relationships. Perhaps, it is his over-eagerness that leaves women feeling suffocated and emotionally drained by his need to be their super affectionate second shadow.

And then, there is G. You can nickname her Girl, Garcelle, or maybe Gianna. G is something special. She laughs sweetly and loves tenderly. In appearance alone, it is possible to overlook her, but when it comes to the quality of her heart that radiates outward, there is no comparison. G is witty, creative, and kind. She is a genuine nurturer who would choose to fall back any day in order to let others shine. It is the purity of her soul that has gotten her messed up by a number of guys who fall somewhere between misogynistic jerks and emotionally stunted mama's boys. Once fed up, G bothers little with categorizing their flaws and instead labels them all fuck boys. She longs for reciprocity, for the opportunity to be loved as deeply, fully, and sincerely as she loves.

Like us, B and G know what it's like to become entangled in chemistry and conversation. When it feels right, we convince ourselves that it's right... even when it's all wrong. We get pulled in by the representative only to be left grappling with a broken heart at a later date. The cycle - this pattern of love and loss - can and will be broken. Change begins with us. Are you ready to begin dating with a destination?

SECTION ONE

UNAPOLOGETICALLY SELF-CENTERED

BREAK UP & BREAK DOWN

What the hell?! How is this shit happening to me, AGAIN? I'm a GOOD woman! These females out here expecting the most for doing the least! Bustin' open stretched out community pussy and still thinking somebody 'bout to drop down on one knee! Tuh! Meanwhile, here I am wasting my time holding it down, being the most real homie-lover-friend he's ever known and he won't even claim me as his girl?! Since when did whores become main chicks, but a man can't see me in his future? WTF! Tell me how I keep ending up with the same fucked up men over and over again!

Again. Once more; another time; in addition; anew. Not many new events occur under the sun. Some find comfort in familiarity, but here we find predictability giving G all the blues! Who unleashed the rage of our little kind-hearted cutie? Yet again, her gentle heart has been crushed under the weight of unrealized potential. The cycle of wonderment, wavering, and wailing has run its course. Again. Things were good... until they weren't. Now, she's drowning in expletives and tears. This time was supposed to be different! Darren was assumed to be the exception to every male-bashing generalization.

He was the perfect blend of high-achiever and hood, just how G liked her men. Darren was charming, patient, and attentive. He captured her heart with lingering hugs and lengthy late-night conversations. He stimulated her mind long before attempting to stimulate her womanhood. Oh, but when he did! Listen! Well, never mind. Think back to your most pleasurable sexcapade, and then, go beyond that. Right! That part. Good girls don't kiss and tell; just know that Darren brought all the goods.

Darren! He told his boys that she was the one and promised to take her home to meet his mama... someday, eventually. A couple of times when discussions about the future came up, he gently pulled her in, kissed her on the forehead, and said, "Baby, tomorrow will come. Let me focus on mastering loving you today." She thought it was cute until she realized Darren never intended for tomorrow to come. Instead, he made her cum to shut her up. He was content in right now, but G at least wanted to consider the possibility of forever. When she pressed the issue, he shut her down with those all too familiar words. I'm. Not. Ready.

Not ready? Not ready!? We've been at this… whatever THIS is… for 10 whole months and he's not ready?! I'm not dragging him down the aisle! All I want to do is define "us" as being committed to one another to potentially work towards a life together.

When nothing changes, everything is bound to stay the same. G fully realizes all the good that she brings to the table, but what about her deficits? Could it be that, no matter how varied the men are, they are still the same because her insecurities dictate her selection process? Before moving forward, G must look inward. Introspection is the beautiful battle she must conquer to experience the forever she desires.

CHAPTER ONE: SELF-AWARENESS

The tendency of most women is to scope out every little flaw when you look in the mirror. Unfortunately, the same doesn't always hold true for looking inward after a failed relationship. Wait! Hear me out. What I'm not doing is blaming you. I am simply inferring that if two people are involved in the relationship, the roles of both parties should be unbiasedly evaluated. Maturity and introspection are required.

When your heart is on the defense, all you can see are the reasons he was dead wrong for doing you dirty. Stop. Dry your tears. Look inward. It is critical that you look beyond him to *really* see you. Go deeper. Reach past the ways in which you were good to him to discover *why* and *how* you chose him. Who are you as a single person? Who are you while in a relationship? What are your values, and do they remain consistent regardless of your relationship status? When it's all said and done, these answers have nothing to do with him but everything to do with you.

Self-awareness is about getting to the root of who you are. You must know, love, and nurture you before attempting to do so for someone else. The better you are at truly seeing and embracing you, the more likely you are to encounter men who are self-aware and capable of reciprocating the love you give. To help the process, I present to you the practicalities of self-awareness:

Self-awareness cultivates empathy.

True enough, everyone is not an empath; however, everyone is capable of empathy. The precursor to feeling the weight of or engaging in another individual's feelings is pulling back the layers of your emotions. What are your triggers? How do negative emotions affect your demeanor? Why do external factors have so much say-so regarding your mood? Understanding how your emotions dictate your behavior helps you to better discern the connection between your mate's feelings and actions.

Self-awareness slows reactivity.

High self-awareness cuts the puppet strings. Being in tune with your flaws and weaknesses works to prevent you from falling prey to the flaws and weaknesses of others. You are more prone to exercise restraint in arguments and not be quick to jump to conclusions. Slow reactivity leads to the clarity needed to strategically move forward in a relationship, or if necessary, end and learn from it.

Self-awareness allows for rapid course correction.

It is hard to stop a moving train. That is unless you are mature in the area of self-awareness. Those who have mastered this ability are able to receive the truth in the form of tough love and then turn compassion inward to begin evolving into a better version of themselves. Doing so equips you to be healthy and whole in relationships.

Self-awareness helps you to identify your needs.

Yes! This is the most important of them all. You have NEEDS! Too often, women go above and beyond to meet the needs of others without taking the time to discover what they need. Self-awareness brings you into a space of understanding your needs, desires, non-negotiables, and unacceptables. When these factors are known, standards can be set. You are able to articulate your wants and needs versus expecting your man to figure out the very things you haven't taken the time to realize.

Guide to Building Self-awareness

Practice radical honesty. You're really good at giving others the business, but when was the last time you dropped some truth bombs on yourself? Instead of setting aside your needs and wants for the appeasement of others, identify how you have allowed yourself to fall by the wayside. Be totally honest with how you feel and devise a plan for ensuring that your needs and wants no longer go unattended.

Sit in silence. Learn to enjoy you! Make time to quiet your mind daily. Prayer and meditation are great ways to connect with the root of who you are. When you come to know and value spending time with you, you will take the steps needed to ensure that your time is also honored by others.

Make journaling a priority. How can growth be celebrated unless it is recorded? Taking time daily to express your feelings in writing creates space for events and interactions to be processed in a healthy way. It also produces an ongoing log of your growth process.

Talk. Often, the conversation in our heads sounds drastically different once it escapes our mouths. Whether it is a trusted friend or licensed professional, talking about your feelings and experiences leads to a heightened sense of self-awareness.

Forget Darren. Let's focus on G. In what ways does she lack self-awareness? How might things have played out if she willingly admitted to herself, prior to entering a relationship, that being a "forever nothing" ranks highly on her list of unacceptables? No matter her past mistakes, every good woman deserves to be loved and valued in her present and to not have her future held in limbo. If you are dating with the destination of marriage in mind, being able to express and stand up for your wants and needs is of utmost importance. This occurs only when you become self-aware.

CHAPTER TWO: SELF-REFLECTION

You're still here. That's good! You now have some practical steps to gaining self-awareness. Next up is taking time to reflect. My working definition of self-reflection is a systematic process of gaining insight from the past to produce dynamic growth that propels you into the future you envision. Basically, look back and learn in order to move forward – better, wiser, and more prepared to step into lasting love. This doesn't just happen. It has to be intentional.

Listen. What you've experienced thus far in relationships ain't it! How can I be so sure? Well, you *are* here. Something prompted you to trust me to put you up on game from a different angle than what has been presented to you before. I believe you are hopeful but also tired. As much as you want to believe that loyalty, intimacy, and security are attainable relationship attributes, you are also battle-weary from fighting to remain connected to men who were content to leave you deeply wounded. You want to be over the notion of happily ever after, but your heart won't let you give up just yet. Good. That means I can be of assistance. Where there is a will, there is a way. Your engagement thus far makes it apparent that you have the will. Self-reflection is the way to begin putting one foot in front of the other to rethink how you approach relationships.

The truth is that until you learn the ins and outs of you, it's impossible to understand how a man operates. Believe me; I am one. There is more to life than going through cycles with men who cannot or will not align with your life goals. Let's be real. Some of them don't even have goals! They are living for the moment while you are building for what is to come. The foundation of *Dating with A Destination* is about being on one accord with yourself before attempting to become one with another individual. Instead of burying hurtful memories, choose to examine and grow from the things you have endured. Choose to reflect on the hard stuff no matter how messy it may have been. In doing so, you are able to release pain, experience healing, and move forward in confidence.

The strength of self-reflection is in transparency. You HAVE to be real with you! Don't even worry about trying to figure out where to start. I'm here to guide you through it. Remember, radical honesty is part of self-awareness. It also plays a vital role in self-reflection. My advice is that you avoid the urge to rush through these questions. Take your time with each one. Search your heart. Feel every single emotion without apology. Get to the root of what happened, why it happened, and who you became as a result of it. I probably don't have to tell you that now is an opportune time to pull out your journal...

Embracing Self-reflection

1. List the reasons your last relationship failed. Be detailed in your answers.

2. Were both parties at fault? If so, explain how.

3. Was the relationship worth saving? Why or why not?

4. What steps could you and your significant other have taken to work things out?

5. At what point in your life did being in a relationship begin to matter. Why?

6. What are the top three areas in your life that you desire change? Explain.

7. How will your life transform as a result of diligently working toward these desired changes?

8. Define the habits, whether positive or negative, that make you who you are.

9. Which habits do you need to change to experience the growth you want and need?

10. What do you really want out of life? Be vivid in your description.

11. Brainstorm habits and practices that need to be put in place for the fulfillment of your dream.

12. With your life vision in mind, how will you choose a mate differently going forward?

G realizes that although she loves long and strong, her love is flawed. She gives and gives and gives before making her expectations known. By the time she is fed up with being taken for granted, her mate is already in the routine of expecting her to be his personal Superwoman. The pattern of her past relationships was dictated by her desire to be needed. What's that about? She was raised as a strong Black woman.

Make something out of nothing.

Work with the little you have been given.

No one is obligated to do anything for you, so take care of you.

Somewhere along the way, this survivor mentality began to mesh with her relationship ideology. Men with potential were enough. Whether or not they possessed the discipline required to live out their full potential was never considered. Her belief was that *she* was enough to make them better. Surely, she could take this seed of a man - whether it was Darren, Cortez, or Xavier - and nurture him to the point of protector, provider, and life partner. G made the common mistake of pouring out the best of who she is without understanding that her heart requires nourishment as well. Now that she knows better, she is determined to not settle for simply doing better. She is putting in the work to be the best version of herself and refusing to expect anything less than the best in her future relationships. Self-reflection helped G to pinpoint what she wants. Now, she understands what she needs.

CHAPTER THREE: SELF-REALIZATION

Wow. *Okay, message!* As a drop of her coveted Apothic Red wine splashed onto her granite countertop, a much-needed aha moment sprang up from the depths of G's soul. *My brokenness is the crack in my past selection process! I couldn't see this crack just like I couldn't see my own!* Another drop splashed. *Ugh! True enough, Darren and the others were on some definite bs. No argument there. Yeah, their nonsense caused the end of us, but MY issues initiated "us."* Well, damn. And there goes another see splash! *Girl, get it together!* G poured her wine into a new glass and discarded the one with the tiny, almost invisible crack. *Let me think through where shit went left…*

Anything built on a faulty foundation is bound to crack and crumble. It's not unusual for cracks to form in the ceiling or walls of a newly built house as its foundation settles into place. So, ladies, tell me this. What is to be expected of a relationship that begins with you settling? Oh no! Don't close the book now. We *need* to have this conversation. You want to date with a destination in mind, right? Then we have to examine the origin (foundation) before moving forward to the destination.

I have enough sisters, cousins, and exes to know that you have or have had a list. You know what list I'm talking about. There are also enough women in my life for me to know that the wrong man can say enough of the right things to make you forget all the standards you set when thinking clearly. Hol' up! I'm not judging your vibe-reading skills, discernment, or whatever you choose to call it. What I am saying is just that like I know, "the list" is discardable, other men do too. When we see you and want you - regardless of our ultimate intentions - we know just what to say to get you. Case in point. There's a reason, after all these years, Mary J. Blige's "Not Gone Cry" continues to resonate with women worldwide. What's your breakup song of choice? Fantasia's "Free Yourself," Beyonce's "Hold Up," Queen Naija's "Medicine," or Jazmine Sullivan's "Bust Your Windows"? The song doesn't matter; it's the continual message that concerns me. Over and over again, good girls - no matter how successful, beautiful, or down for their man they are - find their emotions ensnared in the deceit of bad guys. Why? I'll give you 5 reasons:

1. *She dates potential instead of reality.* It takes more than hope and prayer to transform the heart of a man. He has to want it for himself. Being able to see the good in him doesn't guarantee that it will ever manifest. If kissing frogs hasn't produced a prince yet, it might be time to go straight for the prince instead. Let the frogs jump into and jack up someone else's life.

2. *She dates adult males instead of grown men.* If he is content with a job while you are building a career, you are NOT the same. If he plays video games while you perfect your business plan, you are NOT the same. If he is content to text you all day while knowing that you prefer a phone call here and there, you definitely are not the same! You're out here on your grown and sexy grind. Why waste time with a man who is unaware that life is passing him by?

3. *She dates men who are incapable of dealing with conflict due to unresolved trauma.* Sis, you didn't break him and you for sure can't heal him. I know. It's a woman's natural inclination to comfort and nurture, but he is neither a child to be consoled nor a project to be completed. He is a grown man who has to take personal responsibility

for his healing. You aren't called to be his emotional excavator, digging up the root of every past hurt and wrapping it in your saving grace. You can walk the road to wholeness with him, but you are not his savior. If he wants to stay broken, leave and let him.

4. *She is too future-minded.* I'm not encouraging you to throw your goals out of the window. Yes, absolutely have a plan for your future! Set goals and develop a strategy to accomplish them. Just don't forget how to live in the moment. Getting too far ahead of yourself creates rigid, and sometimes, unrealistic expectations that prevent you from seizing the opportunities that are right in front of you. Be careful to not overlook the one who can build with you due to seeing his present against your future. Let's keep it real. You haven't arrived yet either. A man in process is not the same as a man with untapped potential.

5. *She is married to "the list."* Ding, ding, ding! That right there! Very rarely does life unfold exactly as planned. Relationships aren't much different. Know the difference between standards and preferences. Standards are requiring a man to have integrity, being able to communicate, valuing quality time - stuff like that. Things

such as must be over six feet tall, be a homeowner, and have a credit score of 780 or higher are preferences. Standards are the foundation on which relationships are built. Preferences are like furniture; they are subject to change with time.

I am a lot of things, but powerful enough to make him what he isn't, I am not. If he sees no error in his ways or is unwilling to address past hurts, I am doing nothing more than pouring my love into a cracked vessel. Cortez felt some type of way about my parents blessing me with the down payment for my home as a thirtieth birthday present. Unfortunately, his bank account didn't measure up to the man that either of us wanted him to be. My love fell short of filling the void created by Xavier's daddy's issues. And Darren, well, I don't even know where to begin with him. Scratch that. It doesn't matter. The reality is that Darren was my seventh failed relationship and the first to make me stop and examine myself. Therein lies the issue. Imma need another bottle of wine for this...

Quiz: Are You a Ghoster?

For each statement below, respond "Y" for yes if you are in agreement or "N" for no if you disagree.

_____ 1. Your destination of choice is a good time.

_____ 2. No one feels like the "right" one.

_____ 3. Speaking of which, the "right" one is a fallacy! You need options without a commitment.

_____ 4. Being needed by others is a turnoff.

_____ 5. You two aren't on the same page? Throw the whole book (as in relationship) away!

_____ 6. Friends with benefits should forever remain as such.

_____ 7. You find it easier to stop taking calls and responding to text messages when the chemistry is absent, or when the conversation is dull, rather than verbalizing your concerns.

If you respond "Y" to 5 or more of the statements, you are definitely a ghoster!

SECTION TWO

A MAN'S WORLD... OR NOT

SET STANDARDS OR SETTLE

If you ain't about money, 9 outta 10, I'll ignore you/
It's a man's world, but real women make the shit go
'round...

Aw, hell naw! Not tuhday, Storm...

I take a shot of Hennessey, now I'm strong enough to
face the madness...

Aiight, bruh! You shole know what to say! B raised his glass of Hen
to the sky, saluting the timeless lyrical content of the late, great
Tupac Shakur. The playlist continued on as he leaned back and
let the liquor take effect. *Fuck this shit, man! This whole "I need*
space to think; you're a good guy...blasé blasé" bullshit done got old! Fe-
males these days don't know a good man when they see one! Cheat and
choke 'em out; they love you fa life. Do right by 'em and they need space.
Yo! What the fuck?!

B is tired and rightfully so. The last four years have been spent investing time into trial-and-error situationships, hoping that, at least, one would morph into something meaningful, fulfilling, and long-lasting. NOPE. You see, unlike his homeboys, a situationship was never B's go-to move. The brick wall he continues to hit is that women nowadays expect nothing more. In all actuality, it's the starting point they both desire and demand. At least, such is the case for the chicks he runs across. He longs to tie the knot and live out a family fantasy that was never a part of his childhood reality. But here he is, once again, with a woman who doesn't want to be tied down.

Ladies, tell me. Are you a lover of situationships? Hold on! Before you answer, let me break it down.

Signs of a Situationship

Short-term Goals & Last-minute Plans. Looking weeks, months, and years into the future makes you anxious. Especially when another person's emotional needs have to be considered! It is far easier to live in the moment and not get caught up in thoughts of happily ever after. High hopes tend to result in crushed expectations.

Lack of Consistency. You have become accustomed to consistent inconsistency. When he doesn't call for a day or two (or seven), that leaves space for you to do your own thing - explore a little, consider alternatives. You know the drill. If a man isn't constantly checking on you, then you know he isn't expecting too much from you. And that, for you, is a breath of fresh air.

Small Talk is LIFE. He doesn't know your dreams and you don't know his. That is perfectly okay with you! Again, the future is too far away. Concerning yourself with his life's purpose and motivation doesn't spark much intrigue for you. "How's your day going" or "What's the weekend looking like" are more your conversational speed.

From Boredom to Breakup. Forget spicing it up! When you're bored, you're done. Time to move on to the next thrill. Maybe the next one will be "the one" to keep that fire lit and butterflies in your stomach. Maybe… or maybe not.

According to B's track record, a woman who willingly or preferably engages in a situationship is lacking in one of two areas. Either her self-esteem is so low that she settles for less than a real commitment OR she doesn't have the foresightedness to see a man's current positive qualities in her future. G never wanted a situationship. (Oh yeah. We will always come back to our girl, G.) She accepted these shallow arrangements for the same reason as B: hopefully/maybe/surely, one will blossom into more. Friend, it is counterproductive to desire lasting intimacy without laying the groundwork for a healthy relationship. We have to start well to finish strong.

Before taking your place in the right man's world, let's consider what defines your world. Who are you? What do you need? Let's talk about it...

CHAPTER FOUR: GOOD & GROWN

B basically said that females these days allow good men - focused, driven, heterosexual, ready to commit men - to pass them by. The keyword here is *females*. You see, a female has little more to offer than her anatomy. She lives in the moment because she has almost no ambition to propel her into the future. In essence, she is trapped by something or perhaps multiple things. Maybe childhood trauma, lack of confidence, selfishness - something! A female manipulates men to get her current needs met. She is carnal, reactionary, and desperate in her thinking. I will make this crystal clear to eliminate any confusion. *Dating with a Destination* is NOT for females. This gem is for women - grown women who refuse to initiate or take part in games.

So, I guess now the question is, what constitutes a woman? I assure you it has nothing to do with her bustline, waistline, or educational background. A real woman isn't perfect. What she is, however, is unapologetically authentic among other things…

1. Done with Playtime - Girls play games while women value their present and future time too much for foolery. No matter how fun-loving she may be, she is matter-of-fact when it comes to her moves, money, and man.

2. Intellectually Challenging - Sure, she has *plenty* to say about the latest protective hairstyles and fashion trends but don't get it twisted, she'll also go toe-to-toe with you regarding politics, faulty structures that lead to systematic oppression, and the many ways in which she invests in the ongoing *process* of personal and professional growth.

3. Honest & Genuine - Again, a true woman doesn't come to play. Rather than a masked representative, she presents her true self from the start. In doing so, she not only gives others the right to choose whether or not they want to be in her world, she empowers them to choose wisely.

4. Sincere Effort - Perfect? No. Dedicated? ABSOLUTELY! Women understand that love is more than

an emotion; it is an action. She puts time and energy into learning her man in order to accurately love him.

5. Selective – Few and far between are the women that abstain from sex until marriage; however, good and grown women don't pull their panties to the side on the first date. She isn't a prude, but she is choosy about who she gives her love to.

6. No Ultimatums - Sis is just as respectful as she is decisive. Real women understand that *real* men have full lives with obligations and recreational activities prior to meeting them. She is not at all concerned with vying for the upper hand in their relationship but rather working together to build unity while honoring autonomy.

7. Confident - It's not that she strives to be impressive; she just is. There is an innate sexiness that exudes from a woman who knows who she is. A bold and beautiful self-assured queen walks with her head held high and turns plenty of heads in the process.

8. Honors Space - Women who are good and grown understand that space is healthy. Boundaries are just as important within an intimate relationship as within friend-

ships, work environments, and so forth. She understands that he needs room to breathe... and she creates the space needed for him to do so.

9. Go-getter - Baby girl is a BOSS! She is driven, passionate, and ambitious. A true woman has a mind of her own and a plan for success that is complemented by but not dependent on a male counterpart. No matter the environment, she rises to the top.

10. Determined Visionary - A good and grown woman sees her future just as clearly as her present. She dreams big, audacious dreams, and while she encounters her fair share of hurdles, she never breaks stride while in pursuit of destiny.

In life's stillness is where deep-thinking has its way. G needs time to dive into her thought-life...

In the hunger to share my life with someone, I lost me. I honestly can't even remember when or how it happened. Maybe it was gradual? Did I ever really know me? At this point, I'm not even sure. What I do know is that loneliness and the overbearing ticking of my biological clock pushed me to accept less than what I deserve. Over and over again, I dismissed red flags and gave a pass on my standards. For what? The reward of

*compromising my values was an L every single time. I'm done losing...
done sleeping on me. DONE! It's time to figure out who I am, what I
want out of life, and who fits into my come up.*

Ding, ding, ding! She gets it! G now understands that without
a clear vision for her personal future, the present becomes dis-
torted. She is more likely to settle *in* relationships when having
a relationship is the primary goal. There is more to her than
the man to whom she is committed. As G embarks on the
journey of soul-searching to rediscover her passions and
awaken purpose, she will be all the more aware of the kind of
man who is worthy to do life with her.

I have to ask. G is doing the internal work required for personal growth and evolution. Are you? You still have your journal, right? Good. Reflect on these questions:

Without the roles and accomplishments, who am I?

What do I contribute to the world around me?

Where am I going?

How have past relationships equipped me for lasting love?

CHAPTER FIVE: TO BE LOVED BY YOU

Matchups matter. Tons of women in my life have shared hilarious horror stories about their tragic dating experiences! I probably shouldn't laugh, but y'all be going through! That's not proper English but there isn't a better way to say it. From clueless, good-hearted best friends playing matchmaker to right swipes gone wrong, hopes get shattered when you encounter men who fail to meet your expectations. We men were warned to never trust a big butt and a smile. I urge you to never get your hopes up over a profile. Men lie. There, I said it. The truth is out now. We both know I'm right. We also know females lie, too. Again, this conversation isn't for females; it's for women like you. Social media and dating apps are the perfect place to display an ideal image. Although you opt to post the true you versus a fabricated representative, it is far-fetched to believe that every Adrian, Damian, and Syrus is doing the same.

You can't be with just anyone. That much you have figured out. The question is, who is "the one?" And how do you know how to spot him if he wears the mask that grins and lies? Before considering who you want, be certain about what you need. Relationships aren't a one-size-fits-all situation. Another woman's preference may not suit your liking. Also to be considered is the fact that what's pleasing to the eye may not be nourishing to the soul. Smiles intrigue and profiles lie, but I promise you, personality types are tried and true. Knowing how to categorize men gives you a head start in discerning compatibility. I'm here to keep you with a home-court advantage.

Male Personality Types

Alpha - Think athletic-build with a life-of-the-party demeanor. You will find him surrounded by beautiful women who desire him and Beta men who wish to be like him. Because he has options, being faithful is a struggle. He is competitive by nature and obsessed with his appearance. People-pleasing is his kryptonite. An inability to get his way may result in immature behavior and fits of rage.

Beta - Here we have the Alpha Male's sidekick. He is popular by default and yet unaware that without ties to an Alpha, he falls in status. Beta Males go after the same women as Alphas but rarely catch their eye. They are restrained within their individuality, more prone to conform than to rock the boat. Like Alphas, Betas take measured risks for the sole purpose of maintaining social status.

Gamma - A friend once told me that when her new neighbor moved in, she immediately knew he was no good. Do you have that same built-in bs radar that spots a Gamma Male from miles away? This guy is the sleazy conman who has wrong intentions 99% of the time. He is mildly successful and largely invisible to women. (Females are another story.) Gammas are very much social rejects, but everyone knows it except them. They are overly confident and lacking in social skills.

Delta - Remember B? He's a Delta Male. Top-tier women pass by these men without batting an eyelash. They aren't bad, just average. One thing is for sure: they are as loyal as men come. Get a Delta Male, and he will worship the ground you walk on. Don't be deceived. While Deltas sometimes exhibit noticeable athletic ability, they seldom put much effort into their appearance - as in he's not the manscaping type. They are jaded by rejection, restrained by past trauma, and prone to find comfort in distractions rather than dealing with their issues.

Sigma - Sigma Males are self-actualized. Oh yes, there is such a man! They attract the most elite of women because of their deep understanding of how you are wired. The trick is that these men are slow to give all of themselves in a relationship. Their aim is to keep you emotionally dissatisfied and yet still desiring more of them. This is a delicate balance that the Sigma Male has mastered. He is a strong leader but individualistic by nature. You can expect Sigmas to be both intellectual and street smart. He is disciplined, balanced, and fearless when it comes to taking risks.

Zeta - This is the lone ranger. Zeta Males possess a laser-focus that keeps them in isolation. When it comes to women, they can do without. No, they aren't gay. Instead, they are driven by the tasks at hand and see emotional connections as energy stealers. Unlike most men, Zetas are comfortable with celibacy. Their introverted disposition steers them away from thoughts of love and marriage. Thus, women struggle to gain a position of significance in their lives or even turn their heads.

Omega - Warning: These are NOT the Omegas you went to school with! Instead of tongue-wagging, *Atomic Dog* stomping, imagine the nerd who can probably hack your Amazon Prime account in 2.5 seconds. Women overlook him… until he becomes rich. Omega Males are clueless when it comes to cracking the code of what women want. Social interactions are tiresome. They are typically loners who sometimes congregate with small groups of men who share their qualities.

Before moving forward, look back. Based on the personality types presented, assess the last three men that you dated. Where did things go wrong? How might you have maneuvered the relationship differently? Now, look forward. Which personality type is the one for you? Pray, meditate, look inward - do whatever you need to do before answering that last one.

Maaaaan, listen! This makes no sense. NONE WHATSOEVER! I'm a loyal Black man with no kids and NO drama. Commitment doesn't scare me. To be all the way real, I WANT marriage! I ain't never experienced a real family. I want that! I'm 36 years old and ready to wife up the right one, but yo, she seems nonexistent…

CHAPTER SIX: MARKS OF MATURITY

Wouldn't life be great if age and maturity were synonymous? I imagine fewer women would become jaded by love if it was guaranteed that men who are 30-something, 40-something, or even 50-something were automatically ready for marriage. Unfortunately, your love interest and a Cabernet Sauvignon aren't the same. While the latter gets better with time, the other does not come with the same guarantee. The choice of loafers over Jordans or Jazz instead of Hip Hop isn't a telltale sign. Maturity runs deeper than physical attributes and material preferences. Let's be sure you know it when you see it.

Marks of a Mature Man

1. You are a priority in his world instead of an option - No matter your love language, he learns to speak it fluently. Your presence *and* preferences are important to him. A

mature man seeks to make sure that you never feel neglected.

2. He trusts you with his heart - Ladies, it takes A LOT for a man to be vulnerable. You will know that he is mature enough to receive you as his safe place when he begins to open up about his fears, past hurts, and finances. (The latter is only significant if the brother isn't broke!)

3. His time is a limited resource - A mature man doesn't have time to pass the day talking and texting. This may seem like a contradiction to point No.1, but it isn't. With this man, you are guaranteed to experience quality time that exceeds the value of what an immature man can provide in quantity.

4. He is selective - There are variations of the same meme floating around social media. Paraphrased, they state the following: *Men have sex with who they can but marry who they want. Women have sex with who they want but marry who they can.* In the game of numbers, men have the advantage. We are outnumbered, and thus, can choose to be selective when it comes to monogamy and marriage. A mature man says, "I do," with confidence because he exhibits discipline in his decision-making.

5. Expect him to stand his ground - If you shrink back when being told "No," you aren't ready for this kind of man. Yes, he desires to please you, but his ultimate loyalty is to the mission of your relationship and the well-being of your family and future. That may require him to delay the gratification that you prefer to have instantly.

6. A mature man admits when he is wrong - We, as in men and women, all have blind spots. There will be times when you respectfully point out his error in love. (Keywords being "respectfully" and "love"). At which time, you can expect him to own it up.

7. He is self-sufficient - You're not dealing with a "baby boy." That's for sure! A definite mark of a mature man is that he holds it down when it comes to maintaining his household.

8. He is proactive when it comes to pleasing you - Once upon a time, you had to ask to get your wants and needs met. A mature man is studious, and you are his favorite subject matter. He observes your habits, learns what makes you happy, and makes it his business to keep a smile on your face and an arch in your back.

9. When you are weak, he is strong - We know you're a Superwoman, but every hero needs time to refuel. When you are low, his love lifts you - no questions asked.

10. He has no desire to complete you - A mature man understands that he didn't create you, and therefore has no authority or ability to complete you. Instead, his character is complimentary to your nature. The two of you fit together like a hand in glove, but it's so much more than physical. Your deficits are filled by his strengths and vice versa. You work in unison as a team destined to win at love and life.

All that sounds good, but can you handle it? I'll be honest. Just like good women have been ruined by inept men, there are plenty of mature brothers who have been burned by immature sisters. You probably know some just like I do. Be honest with yourself, do you meet the maturity standard?

Marks of Mature Woman

1. Inspirational - No matter how mature a man is, a mature woman will always inspire him to be better. You are a natural cultivator. Whatever and whoever touches your

heart is bettered by your unselfishly infusing vitality, strength, and goodness.

2. Resourceful - A mature woman stewards her mind, body, spirit, time, finances, and future well. The man that is for you trusts you because of the meticulous attention you pay to each area of your life.

3. Inclusive - You are an open book. No detail is too little or too big to divulge. A sign of maturity is being willing to include your partner in on the ups, downs, ins, and outs of your day.

4. Honest - Transparency and authenticity are a part of your beauty. You keep it 100 at all times, no matter the cost.

5. Balanced - A mature woman isn't overly independent. She embraces the healthy need that men and women have for one another.

6. Wise - You think for yourself. Neither friends and family nor the culture can sway your made-up mind. Instead of being emotionally driven, a woman who is ready for a lifetime love is knowledgeable, decisive, intuitive, and calculating in the life that she leads.

7. Peaceful - Peace, love, and good vibes are what she is bringing all day, every day. Her man is eager to return

home because in her presence is where he encounters rest.

8. Protective - You are the definition of a man's rib. A mature woman guards her man's heart and wipes his tears. He carries the weight of the world outside of the home. In the home, his heart is blessed with the time, space, and love vital for recovery.

9. Respectful - Yes! Disagreements may get heated, but you make it a point to honor your man in good and bad times.

10. Complementary - Just like mature men, mature women do not expect to be completed. They desire men who are ready and able to build a life and legacy... together.

There you have it. You have been presented with a lot to digest; I know. That's good, though! This is how growth happens. Is *he* mature enough to love you correctly? Are *you* mature enough to allow him to lead? Until both answers are "yes," all talks of a relationship should be ended with a "no." It's as simple as that.

CHAPTER SEVEN: 5 LEVELS OF RELATIONSHIPS

Remember how G fell for the "Baby, tomorrow will come" line? Darren hit her with that anytime she tried to DTR - as in define the relationship. Apparently, B ran into the same problem on his end. Both B and G yearn to experience a life of intimate, committed love. They crave reciprocity that doesn't require begging or coercion. And yet, more than a few times, they have found themselves investing weeks/months/years and emotional energy into situationships that faltered instead of flourished. Why? They didn't DTR.

We can agree that emotions are relevant. They serve a role in helping us to process circumstances and connections. That said, it makes sense that they are considered when it comes to relationships. That's okay to a degree. Emotions become problematic when our feelings are granted too much say-so. What happens when a big ol' ball of loneliness, lust, confusion, exhilaration, and frustration rushes to the forefront of our minds? They get a seat at the table of our decision-making and tip the scale away from standards and sound judgment. Thus, the date to DTR gets pushed back farther and farther. Know it that whether the relationship (or situationship) is explicitly defined or not, it still has a definition by default.

5 Levels of Relationships

Disclaimer: The corresponding scenarios are used to paint a picture only. It is possible, but maybe not probable, to experience any of the 5 levels with the different male personality types.

Unconscious, non-exclusive

If you've ever encountered a sigma male, this may have been your experience. He knew exactly how to stimulate your mind, please your body, and elevate your spirit. Before you knew it, mid-week sleepovers and meaningful conversations were the norms. Then, he became consistently inconsistent. Your demeanor morphed into a toxic version of you as intense anger began to rise up over his disappearing acts. When confronted, he said, "But we're not together." That part. He was right. You unconsciously became comfortable without ever addressing the possibility of exclusivity.

Conscious, non-exclusive

You swiped right to ride an alpha man just for one night. Hey, I'm not judging! You are both adults; the sex was consensual. How you get down is NOT my business. Moving on... Neither of you wanted a relationship at the time. You agreed that the in-between-the-sheets-goodness was too good to let go. The fling was on again/off again for a little over a year. You knew what it was: fuck buddies and nothing more.

Committed, non-exclusive

This is the equivalent of loving cookies and cream ice cream but opting for gelato every now and again. An omega man might stimulate your cerebral cortex but fumble when it comes to pleasuring your aroused clitoris. You're committed to Ben but occasionally call on Carlos or Lorenzo to satisfy the itch that Benny-boy can't scratch.

Exclusive, no direction

I don't know how you did it, but you did. Congratulations! You succeeded in locking down a zeta man, but is it really a success?

He agreed to be monogamous. That's step one. Beyond that, he's clueless when it comes to processing the intricate emotions and long-term aspirations of another person. You two are together, but Miss Lady, don't expect much else.

Exclusive with direction

Here stands the delta man. Our guy, B, stays ready for exclusivity. What makes him so different? The life behind him is pitch black compared to the illuminated possibilities in front of him. He is eager to commit and move forward because real love and a healthy family dynamic are things he has yet to see outside of movies.

The mere fact that you are reading *Dating with a Destination* is evidence that you desire a relationship that is exclusive and headed towards marriage. It can also be assumed that your past relationships fall into some of the other categories, which is why you are here. I hope that journal is nearby. Now would be a good time to reflect on how and why vision wrapped in exclusivity hasn't always been the standard.

Never will I EVER again settle for a man who refuses to commit. Man, I straight up gave Darren husband benefits. Did I really do that? G laughed to herself. *Laundry? Done. Meal prep? You better believe it!*

I was out here booking couples massages and pedicures like I have his last name or something! I went above and beyond to prove that I was worthy of his time, of being his girl. But I'm not a girl! I'm a grown-ass woman with no time for games! Huh. No time for games, but I let myself get played.

Okay, G. You live and learn. It won't happen again. I'm doing the work to make SURE it doesn't happen again! Nah. I won't go all-in again until I know he's all in. I still believe in love, but now, I know what love should look like.

Quiz: How to Know if You are a Priority

For each statement below, respond "Y" for yes if it applies to your current or most recent relationship and "N" for no if it does not.

_____ 1. You have met his/her friends and family.

_____ 2. The two of you regularly discuss long-term plans.

_____ 3. He/she puts your needs first without being asked.

_____ 4. You are the first to hear his/her big news.

_____ 5. Spending quality time together is the norm.

_____ 6. There was never a hesitation to commit.

_____ 7. He/she has given you no reason to withhold trust.

If you responded yes to 5 or more of the statements, you're in there!

SECTION THREE

WE COULD BE US

INTRODUCTION

Whatchu know about Reggae? More specifically, I wonder if you're familiar with "Is This Love" by Bob Marley. Allow me to share a few lines with you...

I want to love you, and treat you right

I want to love you, every day and every night

We'll be together, with a roof right over our heads

We'll share the shelter, of my single bed

We'll share the same room, for Jah provide the bread

Is this love, is this love, is this love

Is this love that I'm feelin'?

So goes the narrative of a man who is ready to share and sacrifice for the benefit of the lady in his life. Togetherness. Intimacy. Selflessness. These are trusted telltale signs of relationship readiness, and still, he asks, "Is this love?" My thought is that he hopes to unravel the intricacies of his heart to confirm that he is, indeed, in love and not just engulfed in a fond attachment. Consider the benefit of assessing a connection before labeling it love. Seriously, think about it. How much more fruitful and strong and long-lasting would our "love" stories be if we tested them for authenticity before diving too deeply into a sea of emotions?

Again, we are talking about love versus attachment. The latter is established in how the other person makes you feel. It's that euphoric, on-top-of-the-world-and-don't-want-to-come-down type of vibe. For women, there is no better place than in his arms. You stop waiting to exhale because, with him, you breathe easily. For us men, we stand up straighter, broaden our shoulders, and stick our chest out a little more. We feel like "the man" when our lady looks at us in a way reserved for no one else. Love is inclusive of those experiences and more. Love is truth and understanding. It is reciprocity, peace, and a tenacious oneness that withstands the tests of time. Attachments come and go, but true love never fades.

We have examined the lost loves of B and G, but if possible, I would like to provide a transparent glimpse into my world. Time has taught me that no matter what ups and downs life may bring, there will always be that one person who forever remains in your heart. That one, for me, is Terri…

We were high school sweethearts, and no, it wasn't puppy love. Bonds between military kids are different; the experiences we share abroad bind our hearts for life. Terri and I were instant friends who leaned into an organic progression of serenity, mutual respect, and real love. It was as if our souls previously knew each other. We were like old friends catching up after a long time apart. The world stopped on its axis when we were together. When apart, I craved her smile, her laugh, her touch, and especially her kiss. Our lovemaking was sensual and guilt-less. Every part of us - spirit, mind, and body - trusted that we were supposed to connect. We blended together in a way that made separation feel forbidden. Our love was destined to out-last eternity. From skipping school to hopping trains in down-town Wiesbaden and Mainz, Germany, we did whatever, whenever together. We were the Black Bonnie and Clyde be-fore Jay and Bey.

No secrets, no omissions, and no hidden agendas; everything about us was founded in transparency and acceptance. Terri was my lover and my best friend. Then, life happened. My stepfather received relocation orders and our world came crashing down. Depression took hold of us both. We were lost without one another. Years later, we were blessed to reconnect through Facebook. Interestingly, both of us were married and going through a divorce. Although no love was lost over the years, living far apart posed a problem. Long-distance didn't work for us. Our history was physical, spiritual, and mental. Expecting anything less the second go-round would be cheating ourselves. Terri and I agreed that it was better to remain close friends than to pursue a relationship. But to this day, our love is as real as it was back then.

CHAPTER EIGHT: LOVE'S MAKEUP

What does a professional student and an avid churchgoer have in common? Without life application, neither individual has credibility. Ouch! That's real, though. We can talk about awareness and maturity all day long, but until this new reality is tried and stretched, we cannot be confident in our ability to date with a destination. You have done the work of discovering who you truly are and what you really need. Now, it's time to go deeper into our comprehension of love's layers.

Oh yes, there are levels to this! Unfortunately, society has relegated love to an emotion. That's why we fall in and out of it so easily. More than a feeling, love is a force that penetrates hearts, shifts environments, and leaves lives forever changed. In its purest form, it makes us better. We become less selfish, more gracious, and guarded against the temptation to deceive or manipulate in the presence of real love. We descend into the uncharted depths of intimacy as the sincerity of our love interest awakens us to the journey of two individuals choosing to become one. Love is a choice… among other things.

7 C's of Relationships

Communication. First, you and he are talking. This is the cordial exchange of getting-to-know-you dialogue that seldom breaches surface level. Next is conversing. If you've been saying conversate, please stop. That's not really a word. Anyway, conversing is a reflection of increasing interest. You're thinking, "Maybe this could be something." And then there is communication. Of the three, this reigns supreme. Communication, in the context of a relationship, is the verbal *and* nonverbal transfer of information for the establishment and building of a mutual commitment.

Connection. This is literally the tie that binds. We are quick to say that opposites attract, but every couple has a strand of commonality that links the two hearts. Perhaps, it's their pain points, mutual friends, or their commitment to growth and healing that does it. No matter the case, every relationship has its point of connection.

Compatibility. If you're cool with metaphorical plaids and stripes and he is too, then you have a match! Compatibility does not mean that you agree on everything 100% of the time. It means that your values, interests, and aspirations are complementary, which increases the chance of a harmonious walk into the future.

Chemistry. Sis, you know! I don't have to say much else. Chemistry will make or break a relationship. The communication can be amazing, but if the chemistry (well, lack thereof) makes you feel more like the Sahara Desert than the Amazon Rainforest, there isn't enough lube in the world to make it work.

Commitment. It's simple. What are you building without a commitment? We now know situationships only go so far. The mature man - the man who is suitable for your current place in life as well as your future - is willing and ready to commit to you and you to him.

Companionship. I've heard it said that the worst loneliness is felt when someone is in the room with you. Companionship is friendship wrapped in love. Queen, be with someone that you actually like! Don't be so thirsty that you aspire to be wifed-up by any man - including one that you can't stand. Wait for the one with whom you will enjoy spending forever.

Comprehension. Maybe you've seen this quote floating around social media: *She was an open book, but he was illiterate.* Can I play devil's advocate by presenting that this breakdown goes both ways? Men are not women and women are not men. We are wired differently and that's the beauty of the intimacy we experience when coming together. Identical puzzle pieces are incapable of fitting together. However, get two pieces that know their extensions and indentations are created to intermingle with one another, and the picture is made perfect. Comprehension is a layer of love that motivates you to learn your mate. What makes him who he is? How does he receive love? When he is hurting, how can you walk with him toward healing? Comprehension requires the ability to understand beyond your experiences and predispositions. To comprehend a man is to win his heart.

Excuse me, Ms. Lady. I don't mean to bother you, but I saw you walk in and wondered if you would permit me the pleasure of buying your drink.

G smiled her signature, innocent yet flirty smile. *You know, I'm not big on talking to strangers. So, unless you tell me your name, I'm going to have to pass.*

B flashed a bright, Colgate smile that only intensified the smooth chocolaty goodness of his naturally flawless skin. After shyly looking away, he regained eye contact so intense that G just knew he was reading her soul!

I'm Bryant - Bryant Reese. But my friends call me B.

Well, Mr. Reese, since you had the charm to not approach me with some wack pick-up line, it seems as if I have no choice but to accept your offer.

With me, you always have a choice. G released a cute giggle to let him know that line was approved. *What's your name and what are you in the mood for?*

G's mind raced a mile a minute. She wanted to be hopeful, but she also didn't want to be let down. B was cute in a regular guy kind of way. Even though she would probably overlook him in a crowd, something about him stood out at this moment. She couldn't put her finger on it, but she determined in her heart that she wasn't afraid to find out.

Excuse me, Ms. Lady? We're next in line and I need to tell the barista what you're having.

Oh, I'm sorry! My mind went elsewhere. I'm back now. Sooo, I'll take a tall chai tea latte with coconut milk, please and thank you. And by the way, my name is Giselle. You asked what I'm in the mood for. I know you meant drink-wise, but I'm kind of in the mood for some friendly conversation. Shall we have a seat?

_____

_____

_____

_____

_____

_____

_____

_____

_____

_____

_____

_____

_____

_____

_____

_____

_____

_____

_____

_____

_____

_____

_____

_____

_____

_____

_____

_____

_____

_____

_____

_____

_____

_____

_____

_____

_____

_____

_____

_____

_____

_____

_____

_____

_____

_____

_____

CHAPTER NINE: RELATIONSHIP ALLOWANCE

Before your mind goes off on a tangent, no, this is NOT about demanding a portion of Mr. Right's check! It's about creating a magnetic pull by which openness compels love to find you. Know this: What you allow is what you will experience. You know the negative side of this. Plenty of wrong thinking, wrong motives, and wrong matchups have been tolerated. Times up. The past is the past. Let's move forward into your desired future. In this season of life, you are ready to attract a mature man's love and I am here to tell you how.

The 5 Secrets to Attracting Love

1. Real love sees the up close and personal, desirable, and not-so-desirable parts of you and chooses to embrace you anyway. Allow it.

2. Real love pursues you. You read correctly. The love you deserve will seek you out like a hidden treasure to be discovered. Allow yourself to be pursued.

3. Real love is accompanied by the peace that washes away your doubts and fears. Emotional walls come down as real love steps on the scene. Allow this soothing peace to have its way.

4. Real love abides in truth. Gone are the days of passive-aggressive exchanges and uncommunicated expectations. This love has a voice that echoes the truth for the good of your future. Allow loving truth to be the resting place of you and your man.

5. Real love waters and cultivates you. The end of singleness is the beginning of learning and growing together. It is a process not to be rushed but rather recognized and appreciated. Authentic love nourishes the dry places of your soul while gently massaging your heart back to life. Allow intimacy to revive you.

Soften your heart, baby girl. As scary as it is to surrender, submitting to the unfolding of this process is the only way to experience true love. The pain of your past can only maintain a hold on you if you refuse to release it. You decide when the time is right. The power to attract love is in your readiness to receive it. You want it, but are you ready for the vulnerability that comes with it? Sorry; true love does not exist without vulnerability. I believe you are ready to love again - to *really* experience the love you were created to give and receive. Now, you must trust that you are.

I want to pause to address the elephant in the room. If you're skimming ahead to find out WWGD (as in What Would G Do), you won't find the answer here. In hopefulness, B found G and initiated the pursuit. G had a choice to make. She could recoil for fear of having her hopes shattered again OR she can give B the opportunity to show her that good men do exist. She chose to engage in a conversation over coffee. What happens after that will be determined by the condition of your heart.

The condition of MY heart? Yes, ma'am - your heart. B and G's story ends where your courage begins. If you are brave enough to allow love to have its way, G will be brave as well. If, after all the information that has been presented, you still choose to guard your heart with brokenness and bitterness, so will G. You see, in some ways or in every way, G is you. B, although imperfect, is the man who has spent years searching for you.

Like you, his heart has taken blow after blow. Nevertheless, when he sees you, he will know you without having previously encountered you. He is sure to pursue you. He will invest time in learning to love you. How things turn out will be solely dependent on your willingness to surrender to being loved.

Am I ready?

How do I know I'm ready?

This is a lot!

I'm afraid that if I open my heart to love, then _____,

Those questions and concerns can only be addressed by you and time. Fear stands at attention anytime we go for what we really want. Either fear will have its way or love will win. Again, that decision is yours. What you allow is what you will experience. Distrust can be permitted to reign in your heart or hope can prevail. It's easy to hope that everything works out well for B and G. They are fictional characters whose lives end with the closing of this book. Your life goes on. You get the chance to live what you have learned. You also have the right to toss this content on the shelf to collect dust along with your retired love life. You choose.

We have a little further to go on our journey. You're not getting rid of me just yet! Before we take another step, I want to encourage you. I need you to understand that *Dating with a Destination* was written specifically for you. Now, you're wondering why. Actually, you've probably been wondering why. Here's the truth. I am surrounded by beautiful Black women who have wrestled with the same fears as you. They have cried your tears and felt the sting of your disappointments. They are single and dissatisfied and unsure if love is attainable. Honestly, I'm tired of all of you. I am sick of seeing sisters lose when it comes to love. That's why I am giving you the heads up regarding a man's heart. No matter how thorough I am in putting you up on the game, it won't help if you are content to shield yourself from the possibility of spending forever with the man of your dreams. You *have* to be willing to let love in. Will you allow it?

CHAPTER ELEVEN: THE TRUTH ABOUT TOXICITY

We have practiced transparency this far; no need to stop short of the finish line. It's been brought to my attention that toxic men permeate the dating scene. Okay, that's one thing. The problem is these men aren't single! That's where the confusion comes in. Somehow - with all their fuckery - they still manage to convince good women to commit to them. Notice I said *good women* and not females. Women who are good and grown are tolerating toxic behavior. As one of my Millennial lady friends put it, plenty of women believe a body is better than nobody. Please, tell me this isn't true. Tell me tolerating toxicity isn't the lesser of two evils when compared to loneliness!

I'll be honest. I absolutely do not want to believe that such behavior hasn't knowingly become the norm. Maybe the warning signs aren't as widely understood as I thought, and therefore, the divide between wishful thinking and tolerance becomes blurred. Whatever the case may be, this is NOT what I want for you. With all the self-work you have done during this journey, a no-good man has no right to hinder your progress. Let's take a little time to get clear on how toxicity shows up in a relationship:

Indifferent - A noticeable lack of support and show of approval is a telltale sign. He's blah when it comes to your endeavors and accomplishments but expects you to be his biggest cheerleader.

Unhealthy - Balance goes out of the window, especially in terms of emotions. Toxic relationships have their good moments, but if you find yourself clinging to a few cheerful memories in an attempt to overshadow the negative weeks/months/years, GET OUT. He's toxic, and you know it.

Immoral - Your values conflict. Or more so, his lack of values is in stark contrast to the way you once lived. A person who exhibits little to no moral, ethical, or positive principles deserves your absence.

Noxious - It's no secret that his presence is unpleasant. Soon, friends and family will become distant. Now, his ignorance has produced your isolation.

Contagious - It happens. As the saying goes, laying with a dog long enough and you might catch fleas. Toxic behavior isn't much different. In an attempt to excuse his behavior, you are in danger of picking up some of his traits.

Hazardous - This connection is not at all conducive to your life. His high-risk behavior, emotional outbursts, and lack of regard for your mental, physical, or spiritual wellbeing are all the reasons you need to walk away and never look back. By never, I mean NEVER.

Deadly - Unfortunately, because toxic relationships are so volatile, homicide or suicide are possibilities. We have joked around plenty on this journey, but toxicity is no laughing matter. When you see the signs, do whatever is necessary to sever ties with a toxic individual. Your life could very well depend on it.

We would like to believe that toxic people are easy-to-spot psychopaths, but that isn't always the case. Quite often, they are good people with deeply rooted issues that have been left un-addressed. Just like you are not responsible for their trauma, you also aren't responsible for their healing. I know you want to "fix" him but you can't. Until he seeks help, you are of no assistance to him. Trying to force wholeness on a man who is content to stay broken is like waving at strangers while standing in the middle of the interstate at night. Your kind gesture goes unnoticed because darkness prevents you from truly being seen. It's guaranteed that you will get hurt before long.

If at any time you believe that you're headed towards a toxic relationship, ask yourself these questions:

1. How does this person make me feel?
2. Do I feel safe in this person's presence?
3. Are others safe around this individual?
4. Have I ever felt emotional or psychological distress when interacting with this person?
5. Am I on guard when we are together?
6. Have I ever been caught in the web of their triangulation?
7. Is this person manipulative or conniving?
8. Do I believe that this person pushes moral, ethical, or legal boundaries?

9. Do I feel as though this person adds unnecessary challenges to my life?

10. Am I emotionally drained after our interactions?

CHAPTER TWELVE: GETTING IT RIGHT WITH MR. RIGHT

I have encountered/experienced/enjoyed enough to know that no two women are the same. That good morning smile, those bedroom eyes, the way that thang sits up at attention when you put on your favorite pair of heels - I LOVE it, all of it! I am a lover of women and yet, I know that I am not for every woman. Nor can any other man honestly make that claim. Kima's Mr. Right will vary in personality, stature, and financial status from the men destined to date Keisha and Pam with marriage in mind.

There is no cookie-cutter mold that mass produces good men. We are as unique as you. For this reason, relationship success will never be experienced if you are preoccupied with comparing yourself to others. Your love story has a lane of its own. Whether you crawl, walk, or run in your lane doesn't matter to me as long as you move forward. You know your specific needs better than I do. However, I do know a thing or two (or ten) about what will set you up for successful progression.

10 Attributes of Relationship Success

1. **Be Ms. Right.** Before seeking to build a relationship, build a full life of healthy habits and meaningful endeavors. Learn to be happy solo! The mature, ready-to-commit man of your dreams isn't looking for a liability. Be an asset. His life should upgrade once you step on the scene and vice versa. Make an intentional effort to evolve into the woman you desire to be before attempting to connect with the man you desire to have.

2. **Understand that boundaries are beautiful.** Is an affair a deal-breaker? How do you feel about recreational drug use? Are you comfortable with disclosing the details of your sexual history if asked? Know what you expect and anticipate what might be asked of you. Once the standard of needs, wants, and deal-breakers has been set, be grown enough to follow through.

3. **Honor healthy communication.** You are too grown to initiate or participate in games. Be the woman who says what she means and means what she says. Require that your mate does no less than the same. A sign of

healthy communication is beginning statements with "I feel" and "I think."

4. **Goals and desires matter.** Determine what you have always wanted to accomplish and do it. Encourage your man to articulate his ambitions and then push him toward greatness. Win together! Make the most of your lives individually and as a couple.

5. **Take a proactive approach to all of your relationships.** How we treat one area of life is typically how we treat all areas. Be clear on your expectations when it comes to family, friends, the one with whom you intend to spend forever, and even your coworkers. Remain aware of your boundaries and choose to align yourself with those who are loving, respectful, honest, and committed to growth.

6. **Live from victory.** No matter how you may have been overlooked or violated, you are NOT a victim. Your past has no right to dictate your future. Take control over your present to experience the future you deserve. Allow no room for excuses. Figure out what needs to be done - therapy, weight loss, spiritual healing, whatever the case may be - and do it!

7. **Live with purpose.** This may be awkward at first, but practice stillness. Be still. Be quiet. Look inward. What is missing in your life? How would you define fulfillment? When are you the happiest? Sit quietly and work through your emotions, past decisions, and ambitions. Get an understanding of what changes need to be made to experience a gratifying life.

8. **Expect for love to not hurt.** Toxicity does not have to be tolerated. We are humans; so naturally, pain and disappointment will be felt occasionally. If it's consistent, it's toxic. Nourishing, supportive love propels you forward and restores your hope in life's goodness.

9. **Embrace the start.** True love inspires you to be your best while embracing you where, and as you are. Although he shouldn't present you with a list of demands for commitment, a man who is invested in a future with you may call out areas of potential growth. As a woman who cultivates potential, you will do the same for him. Embrace the beginning while walking toward the future. You and he have a lifetime of growth ahead of you.

10. **Take action.** Love is an action. Show it and expect reciprocity. Assert that love is what is done and not just what is said. Talk is cheap; true love pays the cost of

consistent displays of authenticity. Accept no less than love in action.

You have done the work thus far, so I know you are destined to win. Settling for less than a real man should be a thing of the past. No more dating unrealized potential or existing as unrealized potential. It's time to live, love, and be happy! You are presently becoming the manifestation of the woman you have always dreamed of being. It only stands to reason that you are now positioned to receive your heart's desire in the form of emotionally healthy, forward-focused masculinity. I don't even have to ask. I already know...

You're ready.

_____

_____

_____

_____

_____

_____

_____

_____

_____

_____

_____

_____

_____

_____

_____

_____

_____

_____

_____

_____

_____

_____

_____

_____

_____

_____

_____

_____

_____

_____

_____

_____

_____

_____

_____

_____

_____

_____

_____

_____

_____

_____

_____

_____

_____

_____

Quiz

For each statement below, respond "Y" for yes if it applies to your current or most recent relationship and "N" for no if it does not.

_____ 1. You have met this person's closest friends and family.

_____ 2. When conflicts arise, the two of you make a whole-hearted effort to resolve them.

_____ 3. You are comfortable enough to be your true selves with one another.

_____ 4. He/she feels as though it is important to be connected to the key people in your life.

_____ 5. Both of you embrace tough conversations for the good of your relationship.

_____ 6. He/she never takes you for granted.

_____ 7. He/she listens with the intent to hear rather than just respond when you speak.

If you responded yes to 5 or more of the statements, you are well on your way to authentic love and commitment.

BEFORE YOU GO...

This has been a journey for real, right? I hope that even once you're in a healthy, happy relationship that you never forget the foundation principles that brought you to this point. A relationship is the end of singleness but not the end of individuality. Don't get so wrapped up in him that you forget about you. The same steps that bring you to a place of self-actualization and growth are the steps that keep you constantly evolving into the best version of you. Now, you had to know I wasn't going to leave you without a few final words. When forever love comes your way, don't forget to love and honor yourself.

Helpful Tips

Practice self-love. Face and conquer your insecurities. Learn to love you - flaws and all - before lavishing love on another individual.

Let it flow. What is meant to be will be. Love that is forced is sure to fail. Step back. Breathe. And let the process unfold organically.

Never mold a man. You are a cultivator, but you aren't a creator. Accept that you cannot make a man to be what you want him to be. Molding him is not a part of your job description; neither should it be your volunteer work.

Old habits produce old results. Insanity is doing the same thing over and over again while expecting different results. *Dating with a Destination* is about identifying personal deficits and pain points, and then eradicating those issues. Functioning in newness is work. Do the work anyway! Otherwise, you'll end up back where you started.

Don't be THAT girl. By this I mean don't be the one spazzing out because you are over thirty and still single. More time as a single woman equates to more time for self-development, healing, and solidifying your standards. Woe is me moments are a waste of your precious time.

See it when you see it. Maya Angelou said, "When people show you who they are, believe them." Exactly. Resist the urge to make excuses for people who need to be excused out of your life.

Boyfriends don't get wife privileges. Move according to the level you are on. It is easy to slip into that place of proving that you're down for him. Show your loyalty but don't give too much too soon. Women who practice marriage roles before marriage decrease their chances of getting married.

Know the difference between love and lust. Men get a bad rap for thinking with the wrong head. May I submit to you that women are no less guilty of letting the wrong lips do the talking. Intimacy is more than sex. Give yourself time to be mentally stimulated before becoming physically aroused. In doing so, you will be better equipped to draw the line between love and lust.

It's a process. You're ready... on paper. This content in the context of your life is a completely different matter. Give this new insight time to go to work in and for you.

Make you a priority. Yes, this list begins and ends with the self because that's how important you are. As a single woman, it is easier to focus on you. When your man steps on the scene, things will change. Rightfully so. But no matter what, commit to taking care of you. Prioritize loving you. Otherwise, you will only have fragments of you to offer to him and anyone else. And darling, you have worked far too hard for wholeness to get broken down again by the weight of relationships.

I wish you life, laughs, and lasting love.

Peace.

-Omar

ABOUT THE AUTHOR

Omar Bogan has a way of uncomplicating the complexities of relationships. As a teacher, motivator, leader, and sought-after speaker, he addresses difficult topics and breaks down the barriers between men and women. He restores love to relationships by wrapping hard-hitting truth in practicality. In his latest project, *Dating with a Destination,* Omar's love for Black women is conveyed through dialogue that empowers them to reflect on the past, heal in the present, and attract the real love that they deserve.

Made in the USA
Columbia, SC
21 September 2020